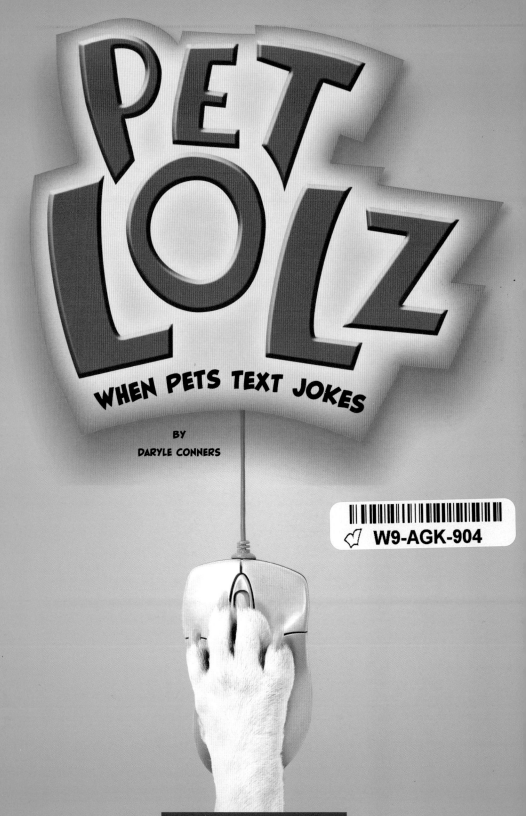

PET LOLZ

WHEN PETS TEXT JOKES

BY
DARYLE CONNERS

W9-AGK-904

■SCHOLASTIC

an imprint of

SCHOLASTIC

www.scholastic.com

Published by Tangerine Press, an imprint of Scholastic Inc., 557 Broadway, New York, NY 10012

Scholastic Canada, Ltd., Markham, Ontario

Scholastic New Zealand Ltd., Greenmount, Auckland

Scholastic and Tangerine Press and associated logos are trademarks and/or registered trademarks of Scholastic Inc.

becker&mayer!
BOOK PRODUCERS

Pet LOLz is produced by becker&mayer!
11120 NE 33rd Place, Suite 101
Bellevue, WA 98004
www.beckermayer.com

Editor: Ben Grossblatt
Designer: Bri Graff
Photo Researcher: Emily Zach
Production Coordinator: Diane Ross
Managing Editor: Nicole Burns Ascue

Unless otherwise noted, all images sourced from Shutterstock.
Contributors are credited below.

Image credits: Front cover: Dog using computer keyboard © Javier Brosch. Back cover: Grey cat and bulldog © Viorel Sima; Computer display © A-R-T. Title page: Dog's paw on computer mouse © sukiyaki. Page 3: Dog with remote © margouillat photo. Page 10: Two funny grey cats © S.P. Page 19: Mouse in cereal bowl © Sascha Burkard. Page 23: Pug © Erik Lam. Page 24: Puppy scratching © Alice Mary Herden. Page 26: Kitty in box © Nadinelle. Page 30: Dalmation © Jagodka. Page 43: Cat with computer mouse © Pressmaster.

Images used throughout: White cat © Irving Lu; Tabby kitten © Utekhina Anna; Cross-eyed kitten © Hannamariah; Exotic shorthair kitten © Eric Isselee; Grey cat © keren-seg; Winking tabby © Tony Campbell; Orange tabby © brontazavra; Laughing cat © Robynrg; Tabby cat © Pashin Georgiy; Black and white dog © ANP; Dachshund © Hannamariah; French bulldog © Eric Isselee; Pembroke corgi © Jagodka; Dog covering face with paws © Ksenia Raykova; Smiling Jack Russell terrier © Fly_dragonfly; Barking dog © Eric Isselee; Winking dog © Lobke Peers; Hamster © Subbotina Anna; Goldfish © Tischenko Irina; Colorful fish © Wiratchai wansamngam; Guinea pig © Eris Isselee; Parakeet © Marina Jay; Tree frog © Kuttelvaserova Stuchelova; Bashful tree frog © Kuttelvaserova Stuchelova; Gopher snake © Eric Isselee; Cute rabbit © Konstantin Yolshin; Grey rabbit © Ninell; Small turtle © Pan Xunbin; Wood mouse © Tsekhmister; Animal footprints pink © mazura 1989; Cute cat theme background © PinkPueblo; Vector technology screen © Mr. Aesthetics.

ISBN: 978-0-545-57261-3

10 9 8 7 6 5 4 3 2 1   13 14 15 16 17

12656

What's the worst kind of cat?

What kind?

A catastrophe!

Where do mice park their boats?

Mice have boats?

Yes, they do. And do you know where they park them?

Nope.

At the hickory dickory dock!

Knock knock!

Who's there?

Howl.

Howl who?

Howl we get away from that dog over there?

How are dogs and phones the same?

Lay it on me.

They both have a collar I.D.!

How do you stop a dog from barking in the back seat?

How?

Put him in the front seat!

Where he belongs!

What did the Cinderella fish wear to the ball?

I don't know, what?

Glass flippers.

That's a good one!

How do you make a goldfish old?

I don't know. How?

Just take away the "g."

Oh! Tricky!

Why did the dog cross the road twice?

Why?

To fetch a boomerang!

Seriously?

I guess you had to be there.

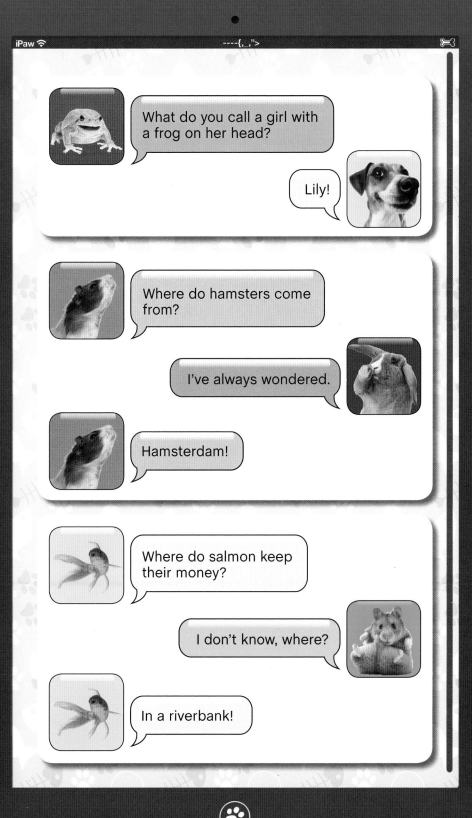

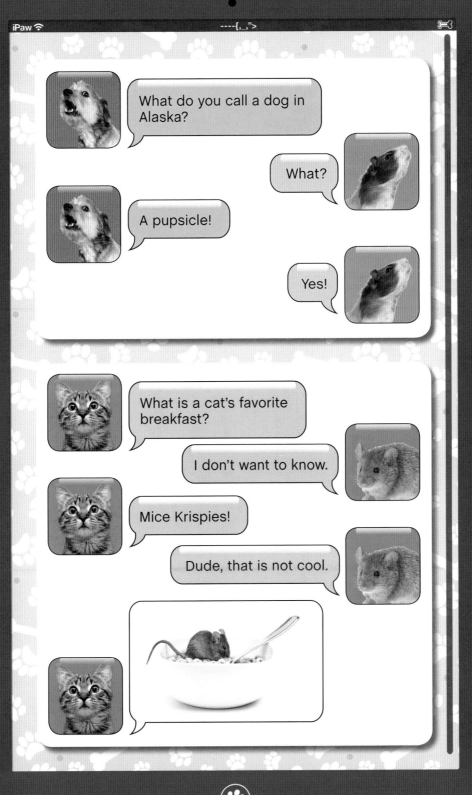

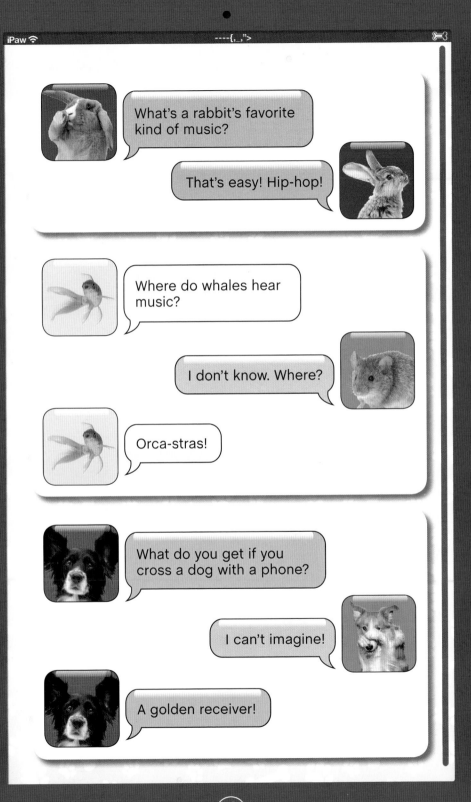

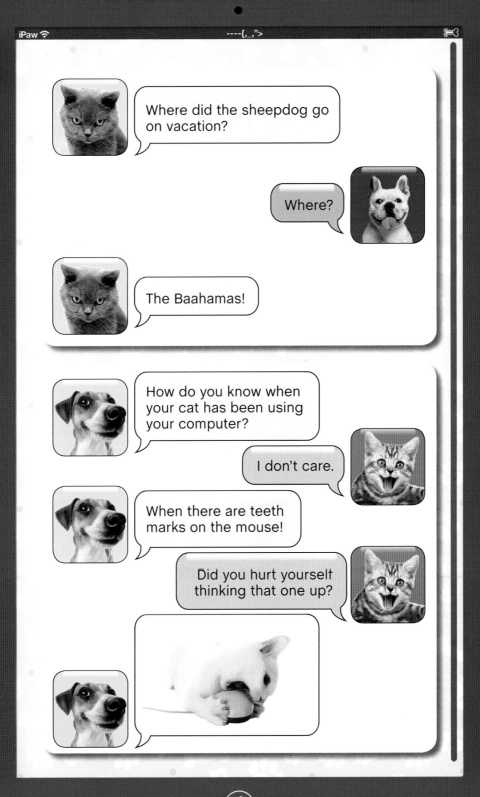

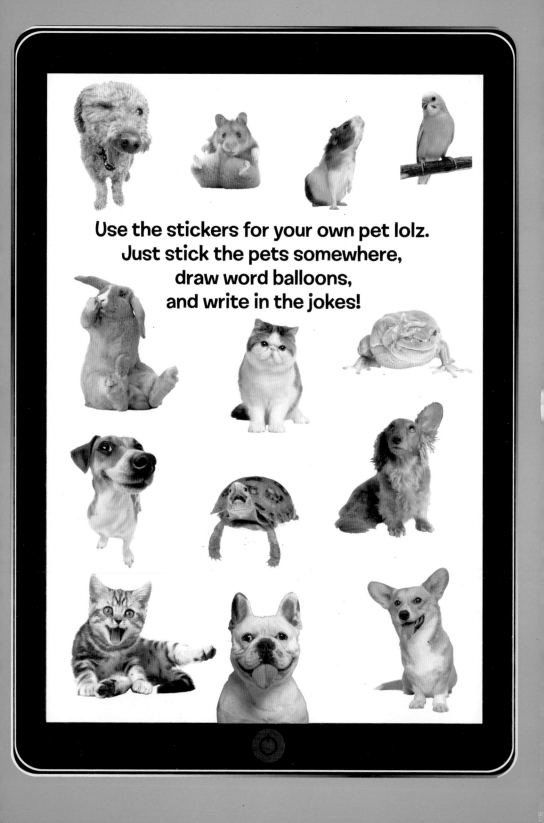